A Gift for:

_____

From:

_____

Date:

_____

ONCE UPON A
Love Song

Inspirations for Love and Romance

DR. CRAIG GLICKMAN

HOWARD
PUBLISHING CO.

Our Purpose at Howard Publishing is to:

• Increase faith in the hearts of growing Christians
• Inspire holiness in the lives of believers
• Instill hope in the hearts of struggling people everywhere

Because He's Coming Again!

Once Upon a Love Song © 2005 by Dr. Craig Glickman
All rights reserved. Printed in China
Published by Howard Publishing Co., Inc.
3117 North 7th Street, West Monroe, LA 71291-2227
www.howardpublishing.com

05 06 07 08 09 10 11 12 13 14   10 9 8 7 6 5 4 3 2 1

Edited and compiled by Philis Boultinghouse
Design by The DesignWorks Group: Cover, David Uttley; Interior, Robin Black
www.thedesignworksgroup.com

ISBN: 1-58229-413-5

Scriptures taken from Dr. Craig Glickman's original translation found in *Solomon's Song of Love*,
Howard Publishing, 2004.

to

John and Claire Hughes

Contents

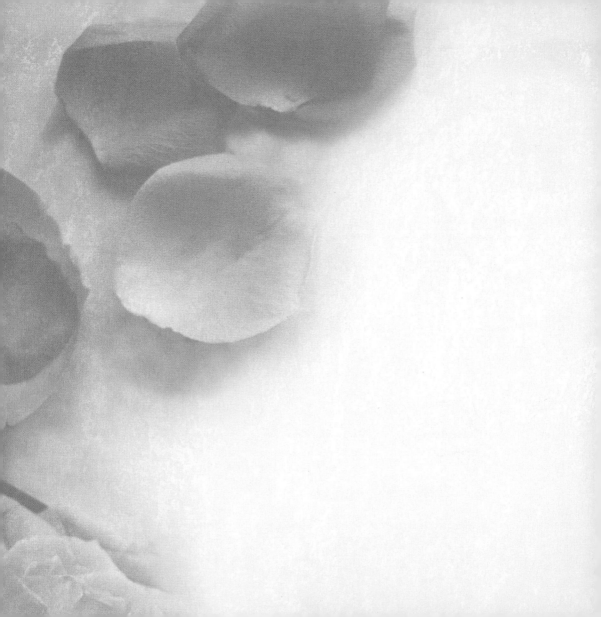

Introduction

The language of love is universal. From the love songs of Egypt three thousand years ago to romantic songs and films today, lovers who speak from their hearts touch ours.

So the best of their words have a timeless quality about them, whether poetry of love in *Romeo and Juliet* or scenes of love in *Gone with the Wind* or a song of love in *Casablanca*.

Their words are not only a literary treasure to delight us, but a reservoir of wisdom to guide and inspire us. They show love's transforming power and the fulfillment it can bring.

The ancient Greeks explained this as evidence that one preexistent soul had split in two to make a man and woman on earth. When these two people found each other, they immediately recognized their "soulmate." It's a picture in myth of the completion they feel.

Perhaps the most famous words of love in history are found in the beautiful Song of Solomon. Written centuries ago, it portrays the essence of romance in the relationship of Solomon and Shulamith.

And it helps us see not just what our partner should be like, but what our relationship should feel like: the role of emotion, longing, and sexual attraction; the foundation of friendship, respect, and commitment; the experience of intimacy, certainty, and forgiveness.

You will find freshly translated selections from the Song in this gift book, as well as stories, poems, and excerpts from *Solomon's Song of Love*, the author's book about this Song.

Enjoy the stirring words of lovers throughout the ages who have seen love break through, who have glimpsed its stunning beauty, and who have captured it in their art.

The best songs let us see love, and the great songs let us feel love. One song, it is rumored, has even the power to instill love. The ancient poets spoke in awe of its name. *The Song of Songs,* they whispered.

Some believe its power still remains. And for those of us who brush time's dust from its enchanted pages, the Song still sprinkles stardust on our dreams.

Romance

To me, you will be unique
in all the world.
To you, I shall be unique
in all the world.

—Antoine de Saint-Exupery

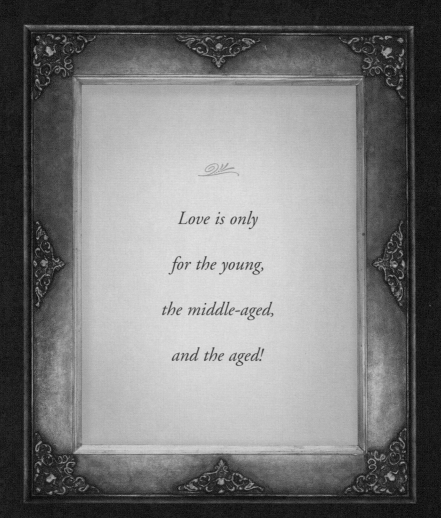

Love is only

for the young,

the middle-aged,

and the aged!

$\mathcal{L}$ove breaks through with a splendor that changes our world. It makes power seem shallow and pleasure incomplete, for power cannot coerce love, and pleasure cannot replace it.

THE SENSE OF THE WORLD IS SHORT,
LONG AND VARIOUS THE REPORT,—
TO LOVE AND BE BELOVED;
MEN AND GODS HAVE NOT OUTLEARNED IT;
AND, HOW OFT SOE'ER THEY'VE TURNED IT,
'TIS NOT TO BE IMPROVED.

—RALPH WALDO EMERSON, FROM "EROS"

"How I wish he would kiss me with the kisses of his mouth."

—*Shulamith*

THE SONG OF SOLOMON 1:2

Once upon a Song of Songs,

Soul touched soul when lovers kissed,

And winter blushed to spring.

Her eyes like his were doves in love,

And hearts like doves arose to sing

A Song of Solomon.

So gentle sounds caressed our dreams,

And wakened gentle wishes dreamed,

And when all hope was gone, it seemed,

Gave us the love that was our dream

From long ago,

When soul touched soul on lover's lips,

And winter blushed to spring.

—Craig Glickman, "Once upon a Love Song"

I had romantic aspirations from an early age, but I got off to a rocky start when I fell in love with a girl who didn't exist.

It happened at the Inwood Theatre, located appropriately on Lover's Lane. Sometime during the hour-and-fifteen-minute animated version of *Peter Pan*, I fell in love with Wendy. She was pretty and kind and not afraid of adventure. Also, she had learned to fly, so maybe she could teach me too. At five years old, I was ready for some romantic adventure!

I smiled dreamily for the next few days, thinking about Wendy. But it was hard to keep so much happiness to myself. So I decided to send her a letter.

The problem was, I didn't know how to write. Mother agreed to help me, and we sat on the front porch and composed my first love letter. As we discussed how best to send it, I saw the solution right in front of me. The trees. Since Wendy liked to fly, the best place to put the letter was at the top of one of them. I wanted to put it in the elm tree on the far side of the yard, since it was tallest, but the branches began so high on the trunk that I couldn't climb it. So I settled on the mimosa tree in the middle of the yard.

I put the letter in one of the empty Mason jars my grandmother used for her homemade blackberry jelly. The jar was waterproof and clear, so my letter would be protected from the weather, and Wendy could see it. I placed the jar on the highest branch I could reach. It was a little scary, but I managed it and made my way down the tree.

I was relieved that Wendy would finally know how I felt about her. When I climbed back up the tree a few days later, my heart beat fast when I saw that the cap was still on the jar, but the letter was gone.

As time went on, I was disappointed that Wendy didn't come to see me or at least write back. But it wasn't really such a rocky start after all. Although Wendy wasn't real, her attractive qualities were. And I learned what I'd like to find in someone who would someday write back. I realized how important it was to find someone who made me feel happy just to think about, to be with, and even learn to fly with.

When love comes, the trees whisper,

the roses exhale their perfumes,

the nightingales sing,

nay the very skies smile in unison

with the feeling of true and pure love.

—SAMUEL TAYLOR COLERIDGE

"You have made my heart beat fast
with one glance of your eyes."
—Solomon

My bounty is as boundless as the sea,

My love as deep; the more I give to thee,

The more I have, for both are infinite.

—WILLIAM SHAKESPEARE
FROM *ROMEO AND JULIET*

Of all the earthly music,

that which reaches farthest into heaven

is the beating of a truly loving heart.

—HENRY WARD BEECHER

Devotion

Love cherishes
the whole person.

Love you?

I am you.

—Attributed to Charles Williams

rue love begins with delight in the whole
person and in the gift of each to the other. It
matures through the journey of life, with the heart of
love beating constant and strong. And it reflects the One
who is the source of all fire.

Love is not love

Which alters when it alteration finds. . . .

O no! it is an ever-fixed mark

That looks on tempests and is never shaken; . . .

Love's not Time's fool, though rosy lips and cheeks

Within his bending sickle's compass come:

LOVE ALTERS NOT WITH HIS BRIEF HOURS AND WEEKS,

BUT BEARS IT OUT EVEN TO THE EDGE OF DOOM.

IF THIS BE ERROR AND UPON ME PROVED,

I NEVER WRIT, NOR NO MAN EVER LOVED.

—WILLIAM SHAKESPEARE, FROM SONNET CXVI

"I am my beloved's, and

my beloved is mine."

—Shulamith

THE SONG OF SOLOMON 6:3

How do I love thee? Let me count the ways.

I love thee to the depth and breadth and height

My soul can reach, when feeling out of sight

For the ends of Being and ideal Grace.

I love thee to the level of everyday's

Most quiet need, by sun and candle-light.

I love thee freely, as men strive for Right;

I love thee purely, as they turn from Praise.

I love thee with the passion put to use

In my old griefs, and with my childhood's faith.

I love thee with a love I seemed to lose

With my lost saints,—I love thee with the breadth,

Smiles, tears, of all my life!—and, if God choose,

I shall but love thee better after death.

—Elizabeth Barrett Browning, Sonnet XLIII

I asked my ten-year-old son if he had a girlfriend. "Yes," he replied.

He was embarrassed when I asked her name, but finally he told me. Of course, I had learned that the next question to ask a boy his age is, "Does she *know* she's your girlfriend?"

He shrugged. "I don't know. I haven't told her yet."

"I see." I nodded. "Why did you select her to be your girlfriend?"

"She's different from the other girls."

"Uh-huh," I said, and paused. "How is she different?"

He shrugged again. "I don't know."

"Think about it," I encouraged. "What is it about her that makes her different from the other girls?"

He thought a minute, then his face brightened. "Well," he said, "if we tease the other girls in class, they all just go tell the teacher and get us in trouble."

I nodded again, thinking I knew where this was going.

"But if one of the boys teases *her*," he said, bursting with pride, "she hits him right in the face!"

"Love is strong as death;

     fervent love as relentless as the grave;

its flashes are flashes of fire,

     the flame of the Lord."

         —Shulamith

THE SONG OF SOLOMON 8:6

In one high bound it [love]

has overleaped the massive wall

of our selfhood. It has made appetite

itself altruistic, tossed personal

happiness aside as a triviality,

and planted the interests of another

in the center of our being.

—C. S. LEWIS, FROM *THE FOUR LOVES*

Love ever gives—

Forgives—outlives—

And never stands with open hands.

And while it lives—

It gives.

For this is love's prerogative—

To give, and give, and give.

—JOHN OXENHAM, "LOVE EVER GIVES"

"Everything about him is desirable to me!
This is my lover and companion."
—Shulamith

THE SONG OF SOLOMON 5:16

Passion

Time together is timeless,
but time apart is an eternity.

I must hear from thee

every day in the hour,

for in a minute

there are many days:

O! by this count I shall be

much in years ere I again

behold my Romeo.

—WILLIAM SHAKESPEARE
FROM *ROMEO AND JULIET*

*N*ew love and spring go naturally together, and the reasons are readily apparent. In spring everything is fresh. New life flows through the world, and a myriad of colors triumph over winter's boring grays. Falling in love is the same. What was black and white is now full color, and happiness triumphs over the melancholy chill.

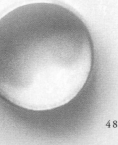

TRUE LOVE IS . . . A LOVE THAT SHALL BE

    NEW AND FRESH EACH HOUR,

AS IS THE SUNSET'S GOLDEN MYSTERY,

OR THE SWEET COMING OF THE EVENING-STAR,

ALIKE, AND YET MOST UNLIKE, EVERY DAY,

AND SEEMING EVER BEST AND FAIREST NOW.

        —JAMES RUSSELL LOWELL, FROM "LOVE"

"Sustain me with raisin cakes
and refresh me with apples,
because I am faint from love."
—*Shulamith*

THE SONG OF SOLOMON 2:5

IF I HAD NEVER KNOWN YOUR FACE AT ALL,

HAD ONLY HEARD YOU SPEAK, BEYOND THICK SCREEN

OF LEAVES IN AN OLD GARDEN, WHEN THE SHEEN

OF MORNING DWELT ON DIAL AND IVIED WALL,

I THINK YOUR VOICE HAD BEEN ENOUGH TO CALL

YOURSELF BEFORE ME, IN LIVING VISION SEEN . . .

AT LEAST I KNOW, THAT WHEN UPON THE NIGHT

WITH CHANTED WORD YOUR VOICE

LETS LOOSE YOUR SOUL,

I AM PIERCED . . . WITH DELIGHT.

—WILLIAM WATSON
FROM "IF I HAD NEVER KNOWN YOUR FACE AT ALL"

I live in a sort of fraternity house, comprised of myself and my three teenage sons. We frequently play touch football after school, gathering some of the neighbors for the game. The boys' school is just down our street, so other students walk past our yard while we're playing.

It's easy to tell when a girl walks by whom the boys find attractive. The first sign may be a football bouncing off a chest or even hitting someone in the face—incidents they seem not to notice, so transfixed are they on the vision of beauty.

Then a surge of energy flows through the players, and they make unusual effort and dramatic moves to gain her attention. I don't think the boys could tell you much about the history of Egypt, but they could show you what it's like when a "mare [is] among the chariots of Pharoah.

It is not time or opportunity

that is to determine intimacy;—

it is disposition alone.

Seven years would be insufficient to make

some people acquainted with each other,

and seven days are more than enough for others.

—JANE AUSTEN
FROM *SENSE AND SENSIBILITY*

The most fortunate couples experience a freedom

that allows them not only to be who they really are,

but also to become who they most want to be—

and to do so while maintaining

a heartfelt oneness with their mate on every level.

"Many waters cannot extinguish love,

and rivers will not drown it.

If a man offered all the possessions of his house for love,

they would utterly scorn him."

—*Shulamith*

THE SONG OF SOLOMON 8:7

A perfect Woman, nobly planned,

To warn, to comfort, and command;

And yet a Spirit still, and bright

with something of angelic light.

—WILLIAM WORDSWORTH
FROM "SHE WAS A PHANTOM OF DELIGHT"

"How beautiful and how lovely you are.

Love flows through your tender affection."

—Solomon

THE SONG OF SOLOMON 7:6

Friendship

Great love includes
not only passionate romance
but also heartfelt friendship.

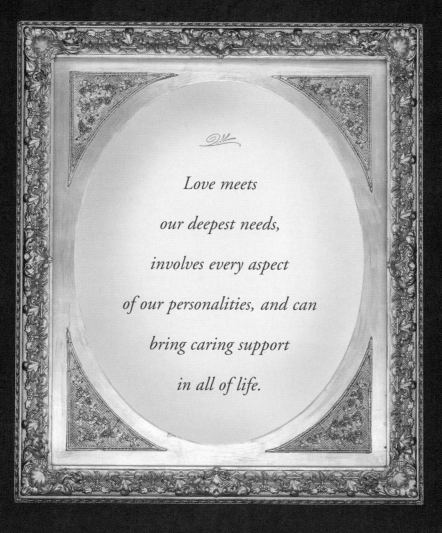

Love meets

our deepest needs,

involves every aspect

of our personalities, and can

bring caring support

in all of life.

*E*ven if preceded by long friendship, love happens in "one high bound"—as though new sight has been given, and for the first time, lovers truly see each other. It may not be love at a literal first sight, but it is the sudden burst of love at the first insight of who that other person really is to you.

My true-love hath my heart, and I have his,

By just exchange one to the other given:

I hold his dear, and mine he cannot miss,

There never was a better bargain driven:

My true-love hath my heart, and I have his.

—Sir Philip Sydney
from "My True-Love Hath My Heart"

"As a lotus flower among thorns,

so is my darling companion among the young women."

—Solomon

THE SONG OF SOLOMON 2:2

COME LIVE WITH ME AND BE MY LOVE,

AND WE WILL ALL THE PLEASURE PROVE

THAT VALLEYS, GROVES, HILLS, AND FIELDS,

WOODS, OR STEEPY MOUNTAIN YIELDS.

AND WE WILL SIT UPON THE ROCKS,

SEEING THE SHEPHERDS FEED THEIR FLOCKS,

BY SHALLOW RIVERS TO WHOSE FALLS

MELODIOUS BIRDS SING MADRIGALS.

—CHRISTOPHER MARLOWE
FROM "THE PASSIONATE SHEPHERD TO HIS LOVE"

When my youngest son was five years old, he fell in love with a girl named Emily. Children must be wiser today than when I grew up, because Emily was a real person in his kindergarten class. But it didn't protect him from heartbreak. She moved away, and all he had were memories, which he often shared with me.

On a day in spring after she moved, he and I were sitting on a park bench on a bridge that spanned a wide creek, beautifully landscaped with flowers, tall trees, and overarching mimosa trees like the one I had climbed long ago. From the bench, looking down the length of the creek, it was a vision of pastels against shades of green that was too beautiful to describe.

My son was the first to speak. "Dad, I want to draw this and send it to Emily."

Then he added, "Will you write something for me at the bottom of the picture?" I remembered a similar obstacle.

"Sure. What do you want me to write?"

"This is real," he said. "Write, 'This is real.'"

He wanted her to know that this world of beauty really existed, even if drawn imperfectly, and he wanted her to experience it.

She walks in beauty, like the night

Of cloudless climes and starry skies,

And all that's best of dark and bright

Meet in her aspect and her eyes.

—LORD BYRON
FROM "SHE WALKS IN BEAUTY"

"As an apple tree among the trees of the forest,

so is my beloved among the young men."

—Shulamith

THE SONG OF SOLOMON 2:3

I have known ne'er a sorrow

That was long unsoothed by thee;

For thy smiles can make a summer

Where darkness else would be.

—CHARLES JEFFREYS
FROM "WE HAVE LIVED AND LOVED TOGETHER"

I give you my love, more precious than money,

I give you myself, before preaching or law;

Will you give me yourself? will you come travel with me?

Shall we stick by each other as long as we live?

—WALT WHITMAN
FROM "SONG OF THE OPEN ROAD"

Fulfillment

True love
grows through
the hardships of life.

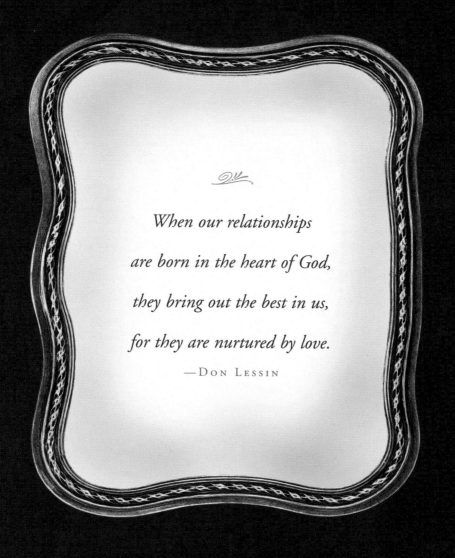

When our relationships

are born in the heart of God,

they bring out the best in us,

for they are nurtured by love.

—Don Lessin

*F*inding the right person doesn't mean we won't face hardship and conflict, but that we won't face it alone. Rather, we face difficulties together—in courage and forgiveness—and we grow closer through it, in the path to genuine fulfillment.

THOU LOVELY AND BELOVED, THOU MY LOVE;

WHOSE KISS SEEMS STILL THE FIRST; WHOSE

    SUMMONING EYES,

EVEN NOW, AS FOR OUR LOVE-WORLD'S NEW SUNRISE,

SHED VERY DAWN; WHOSE VOICE, ATTUNED ABOVE

ALL MODULATION OF THE DEEP-BOWERED DOVE,

IS LIKE A HAND LAID SOFTLY ON THE SOUL. . . .

—DANTE GABRIEL ROSSETTI
FROM SONNET XXVI: "MID-RAPTURE"

"Arise, my darling companion,

my beautiful one; come away.

For behold, the winter has passed.

The rain is over and gone.

The blossoms have appeared in the land.

The time of singing has come,

and the voice of the turtledove is heard on our land."

—Solomon

THE SONG OF SOLOMON 2:10–12

AND YET HOW EASILY THINGS GO RIGHT,

IF THE SIGH AND A KISS OF SUMMER'S NIGHT

COME DEEP FROM THE SOUL IN THE STRONGER RAY

THAT IS BORN IN THE LIGHT OF THE WINTER'S DAY.

AND THINGS CAN NEVER GO BADLY WRONG

IF THE HEART BE TRUE AND THE LOVE BE STRONG,

FOR THE MIST, IF IT COMES, AND THE WEEPING RAIN

WILL BE CHANGED BY THE LOVE INTO SUNSHINE AGAIN.

—GEORGE MACDONALD, FROM "SWEET PERIL"

ow could I have known that one of the most profound lessons I would learn about love would come from eavesdropping on a conversation between my camp counselor and one of the high-school students in our cabin?

"Sharon and I have already . . . you know . . ."

"'You know,' what?" the counselor asked.

"We . . . uh, you know—went all the way," the student said, speeding up his words at the end but expressing himself with a hint of pride.

"What do you mean, 'all the way'?" John pressed, drawing out the last phrase as if to make up for the speed with which it had been uttered. I couldn't believe the counselor was so dense. *What was he thinking?*

"You know, *all the way*," the boy stressed, as if saying it with emphasis would clarify the meaning.

But the counselor didn't let him off the hook. "No, I don't know what you mean. What are you talking about?"

"You know, we had sex!" he blurted out, exasperated.

"Ohhhh, *that's* what you mean," John said with a show of surprise. "And you think that's going all the way?"

"Well, yes."

"That's not going all the way at all," he explained. "I'll tell you what going all the way is. There's a guy in my neighborhood who has five kids, and his wife is now in a wheelchair. He gets the kids off to school each morning, sells insurance all day to make a living, then comes home and makes dinner for the family. And at the end of the evening, he looks his wife in the eye and tells her he loves her. I know he means it, too, because he tells me he's the luckiest guy he knows to have been blessed with her. *That's* what going all the way is."

I dwell on your love through day and night,

the hours I am lying down,

and at dawn when I have awakened. . . .

We will be together even when the peaceful

days of old age come.

—FROM "THE CROSSING"
A TWELFTH–CENTURY BC EGYPTIAN LOVE SONG

"Then I became in his eyes
as one who finds fulfillment."
—Shulamith

<small>THE SONG OF SOLOMON 8:10</small>

Believe me, if all those endearing young charms,

Which I gaze on so fondly today,

Were to change by tomorrow, and fleet in my arms,

Like fairy gifts fading away,

Thou wouldst still be ador'd,

as this moment thou art,

Let thy loveliness fade as it will,

And around the dear ruin,

each wish of my heart

Would entwine itself verdantly still.

—THOMAS MOORE
FROM "BELIEVE ME, IF ALL THOSE ENDEARING YOUNG CHARMS"

The Song of Solomon tells of a Great Songwriter who wants us to know the joy of love—who wants us to reach out in love bravely; who stands by to catch us if we fall; and who yearns for us to know the heartfelt love of our dreams.

If you listen closely, you may hear his music, or even his voice, whispering hope on the way. In the sounds of the wind rustling leaves on a picnic, in the song of the wind whistling notes through the trees, in the breath of the wind bearing fragrance of the sea, you may sense him gently urging: *Fly on these winds. Fly like the doves, through the leaves, over trees and the sea. Let your heart feel the ways of love.*

"The most fascinating book I've ever read on the Song of Songs."

—Dr. Henry Cloud, psychologist and author

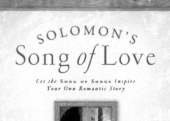

SOLOMON'S
Song of Love

*Let the Song of Songs Inspire
Your Own Romantic Story*

*Sometimes, just when you least expect it,
love gives you a dream come true.*

DR. CRAIG GLICKMAN

FOREWORD BY DR. HENRY CLOUD

The beautiful book you hold in your hand is just a sampling of the rich content you'll find in the author's full-sized book, *Solomon's Song of Love*. With delightful simplicity, Dr. Craig Glickman unveils the mystery of the passionate biblical book, Song of Solomon, and reveals its breathtaking vision of passionate love.

Whether you're a romantic, a scholar, or both, this book will give you new insights into the oldest language of all—the language of love.

Also included in this book—a fresh, original translation of that ancient Song by Dr. Glickman.

Author Craig Glickman holds a BA in philosophy, a ThM from Dallas Seminary, a doctorate in biblical studies and philosophy, and a Doctor of Jurisprudence. As a renowned biblical scholar, his original translation of the Song of Solomon has received resounding accolades. For more information visit www.craigglickman.com.

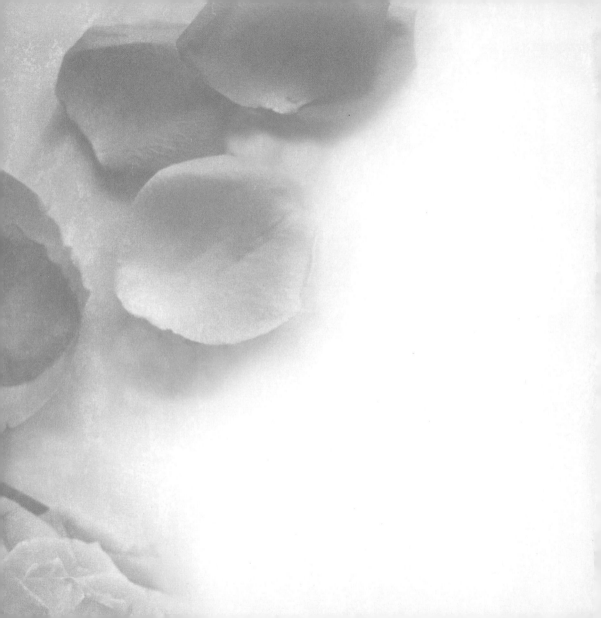